JC
15

8-02

D0881813

THE BEFORELIFE

THE BEFORELIFE

Poems by

FRANZ WRIGHT

Alfred A. Knopf
New York
2002

www.randomhouse.com / knopf / poetry

Knopf, Borzoi Books, and the colophon are
registered trademarks of Random House, Inc.

Grateful acknowledgment is made to the following
publications, in which a number of these poems previously
appeared: *Can We Have Our Ball Back?*, *Conduit*, *DoubleTake*,
Field, *The New Republic*, *The New Yorker*, and *Slope*.

Library of Congress Cataloging-in-Publication Data
Wright, Franz, [date]
The beforelife : poems / by Franz Wright.
p.   cm.
ISBN 0-375-70943-6 (trade pbk.)
1. Narcotic addicts—Rehabilitation—Poetry.   2. Drug abuse—Poetry.   I. Title.
PS3573.R5327 B44 2001
811'.54—dc21   00-042854

Manufactured in the United States of America
Published January 31, 2001
First paperback edition, April 11, 2002

*I wrote these poems
between December of 1998
and December of 1999
for my wife Elizabeth.*

F.W.

CONTENTS

Thus in the pursuit of consciousness it must be understood, first, that man must do everything by himself—that is, he must penetrate to another level solely by his own efforts; and second, he can do nothing by himself—that is, his whole endeavor must be to contact higher sources and levels of energy. For unless he succeeds in so doing, he will get nothing and can get nothing.

Rodney Collin

THE BEFORELIFE

EMPTY CATHEDRAL

There's this pew
at the back
that's been
waiting
for you
all your life, like your death bed.
Christ Criminal
hanging
above, eyes and mouth
closed suggesting
before you too enter
the third person, light
one candle
for the here,
will you.

PRESCRIPTION

While you lie in bed
watching the movie
of every last terrible
thing you have done, you

consider with high admiration
and envy the one
of unscared face
and conscience come

with his own slip of paper
proclaiming
bearer's incontrovertible
privilege to sleep,

to ask
and receive it
right now
by sidereal name.

TRANSLATION

Death is nature's way
of telling you to be quiet.

Of saying it's time
to be weaned, your conflagration starved
to diamond.

I'll give you something to cry about.

And what those treetops swaying
dimly in the wind spelled.

NOVEMBER 14

After church we had breakfast at a diner nearby,
and when we got home provided a poor squirrel
in our street with a burial: cardboard box, plastic bag,
garbage can at the curb. He was perfect,
a large, unmolested and sleeping-appearing squirrel
with a little brilliant dark blood at its nostrils
and the wind slightly lifting the gray and black hair
on its tail and inside its small ear to make me cry.

MEMOIR

Just hope he forgot the address
and don't answer the phone

for a week:
put out all the lights

in the house—
behave like you aren't there

if some night when
it's blizzarding, you see

Franz Wright arrive
on your street with his suitcase

of codeine pills,
lugging that heavy

black manuscript
of blank texts.

WRITTEN WITH A
BASEBALL BAT—SIZED PENCIL

You can meet them all
here, these are the people
who aren't coming back:
the young woman who lives in the room
across the hall, the pretty blonde
who enters in a speechless rage
to leaf through your suitcase
while you're lying in bed and deny it
when asked why, deny
that she is there at all ("—don't go
telling tales on *me*").
The teenage stroke victim
who keeps stuffing his clothes
in his mother's hamper
at home, the black plastic
refuse container
in the bright sterilized
kitchen we're barred from when hungry
between feedings, coming back
to do it again
each time they're returned to him. Then
there's the seventy-year-old manic virgin
who is having a hard time taking her eyes off
your ass, mooning after you, floating
downhall
behind you wherever you turn—

you can laugh
until your heart stops, nothing's
capable of persuading her
you aren't the answer to her prayers;
who secretly opens your door
a crack in the blackness, she stays up all night
gazing cadaverously down
or she would
if it weren't for the guy in white come
on the half hour shining
his flashlight in your open eyes to see
if you've killed yourself yet. And who knows,
you might be one of them
yourself
by now, stranger
things have happened—

NOT NOW

for Dzvinia Orlowsky

Where is
the man of heaven
in me—

my body's
filthy,
face and hands

completely filthy
with
the man of dust

This mask
this glove
of human flesh

is all I have
and that's not bad
and that's not good

not good enough

not now

THE DEAD DADS

It's easier to get a rope
through the eye of a needle than
the drunk son of a drunk

into stopping
into waking—oh no, not
this guy, he's intent on

finding out and finding out
exactly
what the poor old fucker felt like

and hell,
all he has asked
is one good cold responsible

look at the corpse
when it meets him, living,
at the door— . . .

THE MIDNIGHT SNACK

It was night, I was
having a fairly nice time
for a cockroach

in a psychiatrist's kitchen—
chewing in the blackness,
a terrified but unmolested listening.

A bargain,
I remember thinking,
at twice the price I paid;

perhaps I shall injure myself
and require an injection for pain.
A hungry ghost at any age.

But it was night, and it would be
for the time being,
I was doing all right.

I'M SORRY

Child I helped
to do away with

you would be
almost an adult now

I hope my friend

Like me you never got to have your childhood
You never even got to exist
yet

you still bear the name
I gave you
again for my benefit
mindlessly
after your death
your cheap and meaningless
banishment
forgive me

THE ASCENT OF MIDNIGHT

Sometimes I'd like to give up—
I want to blindfold this head
put a gun to it, and say
shitface
this is the way
you caused me to feel
nearly all the time.
But what is the use of that type
of behavior. I'm getting so tired, and I'm nowhere
nowhere near
my illustrious friends (yet
I'm still fairly high
in the mountains
beneath the sea . . .)

BODY BAG

Like the condom in a pinch one size fits all.

THE BEFORELIFE
for Thomas Lux

Meanwhile,
I visit the word world.

In between feeding my friends,

the alert preternaturally unafraid
birds
of Purgatory Cove.

THANKS PRAYER AT THE COVE

A year ago today
I was unable to speak
one syntactically coherent
thought let alone write it down: today
in this dear and absurdly allegorical place
by your grace
I am here
and not in that graveyard, its skyline
visible now from the November leaflessness
and I am here to say
it's 5 o'clock, too late to write more
(especially for the one whose eyes
are starting to get dark), the single
dispirited swan out on the windless brown
transparent floor floating
gradually backward
blackward
no this is what I still
can see, white
as a joint in a box of little cigars—
and where is the mate
Lord, it is almost winter in the year
2000 and now I look up to find five
practically unseeable mallards at my feet
they have crossed
nearly standing on earth they're so close

looking up to me
for bread—
that's what my eyes of flesh see (barely)
but what I wished to say
is this, listen:
a year ago today
I found myself riding the subway psychotic
(I wasn't depressed, I wanted to rip my face off)
unable to write what I thought, which was nothing
though I tried though I finally stopped trying and
　　　　　looked up
at the face of the man
directly across from me, and it began
to melt before my eyes
and in an instant it was young again
the face he must have had
once when he was five
and in an instant it happened again only this
　　　　　time
it changed to the face of his elderly
corpse and back in time
it changed
to his face at our present
moment of time's flowing and then
as if transparently
superimposed I saw them all at once

OK I was insane but how insane
can someone be I thought, I did not
know you then
I didn't know you were there God
(that's what we call you, grunt grunt)
as you are at every moment
everywhere of what we call
the future and the past
And then I tried once more
experimentally
I focused
on another's face, no need to describe it
there is only one
underneath
these scary and extremely
realistic rubber masks
and there is as I also know now
by your grace one
and only one person on earth
beneath a certain depth
the terror and the love
are one, like hunger, same
in everyone
and it happened again, das Unglück geschah
you might say nur mir allein it happened
no matter who I looked at

for maybe five minutes long enough
long enough
this hidden trinity
I saw, the others
will say I am making it up
as if that mattered
Lord,
I make up nothing
not one word.

ACCEPTING AN AWARD

A voice
neither cruel nor benevolent
said—this
was spring
in 1996—
look at him:
he can't live and pretends
he is going to die . . .

One eye in tears and one that's never going to cry.

And who could have foreseen
I'd outevil them all,
all my old
evil friends
put together?

You,
that's who.

Stupid, stupid, stupid, stupid, stupid
and her boyfriend Why
why, why.

So welcome back.

How have you been.

And for this immense pleasure and honor
what will I owe this time—?

ADDRESS SEARCH

And you will find me
any night
now, try
at the motherless sky.
com

How dare you
interrupt
me.com

I'm sorry
I was ever born.com

No doubt
you can always find
me any
time, any
where

in the damned world

BASED ON A PRAYER OF RABI'A AL-ADAWIYYA

God, if I speak my love to you in fear of hell, incinerate me
in it;
if I speak my love to you in hope of heaven, close it in my face.
But if I speak to you simply because you exist, cease
withholding from me your
neverending beauty.

Rabi'a al-Adawiyya was an early Sufi poet. She died in 801.

Formerly
in the first forests it was strange
if you happened
to run into somebody
you did not know; now
it is so strange meeting
someone you do.

THE NEIGHBOR
from Rilke

Strange violin, is that you?
In how many distant cities now
has your lonely night spoken to mine?
Do hundreds play you—or only one?

Are all the great cities occupied
by somebody who, but for you,
would have long disappeared in the river?
And why is this constantly happening,

why am *I* always the neighbor of those
who out of their own dread compel you to sing
and say: this life is heavier than
the heaviness of all things combined.

THE WEDDING

As in heaven
all are smiling
at you, even
those
who know you.

ENTRY & PRAYER
for Gail Whitney

When you get tired of reading
all the beautiful words
by lousy human beings, and come to

the end of your patience with the voluminous
indeed inexhaustible
mediocrities of goodness,

what to do? I suggest—
I don't know.
Let him think.

And if there are no words

to this place give him back
the illiterate sleep: no need
the haldol needle night-night;

let him go quietly, not
in horror,
not in glory.

THE POEM SAID

The poem said never love anything
Not even you?
I asked
and it answered

especially me

If you must, love

not living
with hope

or not living

taste this
and remember

not yet being—

Especially me

I am just you

If you must, like
and coldly admire my cold stars
shit for brains

love what I stand for
not me

the leopard the beautiful
death
who puts on his spotted robe when he goes
to his chosen,
the

what was the not now the what will be

Like suddenly using a dead friend's expression

Make yourself useful
while there is time

while there is still light and time

NEW PAGE

Snowfall a perpetual soft
January snowfall

covers your tracks, and what follows

the period
left
by the needle

DOING A LINE OF OLGA BROUMAS

It is my job to be ill.
—*Bernadette Soubirous*

It's not the wolves it's the sheep

Yes

And it's not the children

Bless your night

If I knew
now
what then
I knew

Night in one eye
                    struck by sleep,

the nineteenth Apparition . . .

Bless your light

COMMUNION

This morning I saw them again
I was just going to tie off
the garbage bag
and there they were
I'd heard of them!
the upper .5%
wealthiest maggots

You do not have because
you do not ask
you do not ask
because you do not have

Last night I lay in my mother's back yard, a
forest
listening to its bird—

Patient shall hereby refrain
from further experimentation
with the windshield wipers
and various rock & roll stations

This morning I watered the flower, extremely
impressive in a monster

Here's one for you, Why does F drink
(Gives him something to do
after he shoots up)

Time to begin

slimming down
for the eye of the needle

Time to see the world without
the special glasses
oh light,

I had forgotten

Rats prefer it to food

AFTER APOLLINAIRE

for Eric Lorberer

It's four o'clock in the afternoon,
and it is finished;
I sit back and light my cigarette
on a ray of dusk.
I don't want to write anymore.
All I want to do is smoke.

I FOR ONE

I for one never asked
for my youth back; when I was young
I was always afraid.
Like somebody in a war

with no allegiance
I was terrified
of everyone.
But now

now I am amazed
and grateful every day.
I don't know how that happened.
I am so glad

there is no fear,
and finally I can

ask no second life.

DESCRIPTION OF HER EYES

Two teaspoonfuls,
and my mind goes
everyone can kiss my ass now—

then it's changed,
I change my mind.

Eyes so sad, and infinitely kind.

TIBETANS RAPED BY CHINESE ROBOTS

Bill Knott traveling
stripped
self-stripped of all earthly possessions
save a childhood lamp
which he carries
I'm told by a sad girl who slept
with him, or would have
from one desolation to another
in rooms across
Manhattan
winter,
1979?

FROM A DISCARDED IMAGE

The world's wordless beauty's
intact and can never be other than
intact no matter what
harm we perpetually do
and have done
and will I can assure everyone
do,
forever,
as they say

World's wordless beauty, and the word's
worldless liberty

The champagne shopping binge
                is over
The check is about to arrive
and nobody knows how much it will be
I know I don't give a shit   not now

The world's
wordless
beauty intact, indeed

it can never be other
than

radiantly intact
like the stars, like the stars

when the stars have no names once again.

SELF-PORTRAIT AT 40

He's not in the hospital now
the hospital's in him,
it's everywhere

like the sky
all his poor
friends lining up
for their little white paper
shotglasses
filled with pills

yearlong instants of fear
and clinical paranoia
at the water fountain
in second grade

already deceitful obsequious the book reduced to writing

At times he's inspired
intense desire
to heal him in women
and then
a bit later
to kill him

A strangerness
that will always be with him
sometimes
cruel
and often funny
scared to death
every so often
for days on end,
however
Engaged

between one
December
and another
and another

perpetual gift

He will be buried with
a little gold

cross hanging from his neck
pulling him down

and lifting him up—
truly

    there is no down
or up where he is going, bright
gold gleaming in the earth
the sun

still shining in it
at the moment . . .

Just say
he wished to do something
that would make his friends glad
and his enemies sick, and
there was apparently nothing
he could do about it, and nobody

    can tell you why

SCROLLING MARQUEE

Broken-necked sunflower
in my dusk wind glowing
Like reading the *Iliad*

to a blind child . . .

No, Friday's out, Franz
how about never
is never good for you

is sleep to me burning is sleep to me burning

Harmless, unless
he takes a liking to you

I never do get caught, it's very odd

BATHTUB IMPROV

Book composed of poems no one will ever read
or write, if I can help it:
each verse composed of words
I will never cleverly jot,
or transcribe from memory, never
recite in my blood—
e.g., the jagged sonnet which begins
For sure the motherfucker's sober now—
book with hunter
green cover, the beautiful color
of oak leaves in summer,
with no smirking photograph;
color of life, color of death
with no prizes, no trivial biography, no academic
honors earnable by any moron who can read
or write his name. No name
or gloating progeny
of shame, no irrelevant
lies and not one
date.

RESURRECTION: ELEGY

In San Francisco John Logan said, light
is the shadow of God
and
have you ever tried
Green Chartreuse

What do you mean
you've never heard
Mahler's 2nd Symphony

Sent me long before that
friendly evening meeting
under the Bridge
one gray northern Ohio winter day
the great Glenn Gould and Roxolana Roslak *Das Marienleben*
right before
my translation came out

who could barely open his eyes,
and politely
drank himself to death

yet met me the summer
after you died
his dead friend's
son
he treated me
one glorious last champagne and tequila-fueled
supper and led me then
no doubt by heart
in the streets
to the vast golden house of this music

SIMULTANEOUS SENTENCES

Only diamonds can cut diamonds, though
to do any such thing
they have no wish

The ghosts don't believe in us

GOODBYE

But I have overcome you
in myself,
I won't behave

like you, so you

can't hurt me now;

so you are not
going

to hurt me again

and I, I can't
happen
to you.

SLANDER

I can just hear them
on the telephone and keening
all their kissy little knives

or voraciously taking turns
nursing a lie
still in its early white whisperhood

and I could do something
bad back to them
someday, I guess—

but why

Exclusion doesn't hurt
that much, in fact

I've visited the stars on foot

Come disdain of the dreamhand for grammar
and fame, this Boston's
gothic chilly April
night (new leaves the color
of her eyes) beloved

booknight *real*
real world, oh
prasini arachni
s'agapo

Light green eyes dusk distant
tolling now fading
to heartscar
which says

I was loved, always
loved

And then they wounded me
                              so usefully

AESTHETIC

The instant before
the slash bleeds—
for example

her hair getting long like the night in late fall.

Kayaking alone on Lake Kakapoopee.

Crown of barbed wire, no one is born sad.

I owe you so much—
I owe you my life.
I would have killed myself
five different times, had it
not been for the thought of
your intense secret pleasure
while you wept at my grave.

I would go hiddenly,
write in rage: when she smiles
she looks just like a knife blade—
know what I mean.
In *my* mind, I was already dead; now

I am alive again
and it is you
who're deceased, despite appearances
and I like this
so much better.

To tell you the truth.

THE SPEAKER

Who worked his fingers to the ghost,
and for what

Words will be over, then: soon
he'll be silenced,
and said.

CHURCH

Lantern cabin,
Arkansas

organ
beating
bass

Wind, dark
and wind
bird

tiny dark

startled
eye.

COMMERCIAL FOR ABSENCE

Try it,
just a touch
of being noplace

at the pulse points.

And I'm not
mad (when I'm mad

you will know it)—

I am here, and I'm not
angry with anyone.

Can't you sense it.

I'm here, and I'm not.

THINKING OF FRANCE
from Celan

Think along with me: Paris sky, spacious eternity of fall.
From the flower girl we bought these hearts:
they were blue and bloomed in water.
It started raining in our room
and the neighbor came over, Monsieur Le Songe, a haggard
little man.
Then we played poker, I misplaced my pupils;
you let me wear your hair, I lost it, he depressed us.
He walked through the door, the rain following.
We were dead and could still breathe.

THE WAY WE LOOK TO THEM

Though perhaps when I thought you were looking away
you, too, were wishing
not to be seen; when
I thought you were looking at me
with coiling sneer, or pity, maybe
you too with your eyes
were beseeching
to be seen,
friend—

THE MIRACLE

You mean I am not an automaton
subject
to his most thoughtless whim? You mean
all this isn't his dream?
She mixed tears with a little dirt, and
                applied it to her eyes—
suddenly she was seeing.
And then she was not going back there
tomorrow, so
nothing could stop her.

REQUEST

Please love me
And I will play for you
this poem
upon the guitar
I myself made
out of cardboard and black threads
when I was ten years old.
Love me or else.

HOMAGE

There are a few things I will miss,
a girl with no shirt on
lighting a cigarette

and brushing her hair in the mirror;
the sound of a mailbox
opening, somewhere,

and closing at two in the morning
of the first snow,
and the words for them.

TO A BLOSSOMING NUT CASE

Why isn't Jesus' face ever described?

Because
in heaven unlike earth
it doesn't make a difference
what one looks like,
I suppose

face up
on the motel bed

And yes I've seen
my records
in three manila volumes
thick as the Boston white pages
It looks like a suitcase
you can't get to close
it looks like a bed that hasn't been made
in over a year

Face
up on the grubbled sea
of this infected unfamiliar
and infinite room, the sheet
tenting my nose

the toilet filled with blood

And I almost forgot
is my mind in this
room or this room
in my mind
all in my mind

Dark the computer dies in its sleep

LEARNING A LANGUAGE

She's reading your minds
as you pass by, the

dipsomane déguisée en rose

While she waits
for her date
to turn up, the moon
in the man . . .

She knows exactly what is going to happen

she'll be guided
upstairs
to a bedroom, and turning around
he will show her his
gun

He'll ask if she would like to
hold it,
which she will

amazed
at its lightness

and beauty
this thing

it must have taken 4 million years to make

squeezing it she will feel cold
and invisible light flowing
into her spine

So there is a door out of here after all

And to visit a new place creates one
in the brain

How do you say no

How do you say anything
to throw up in

Can I use this room to cry

Radiant fuel
body
of water

along which she walks, she is
walked

Why
did we leave, and how
are we ever getting back—

FINE PRINT

Look at the hand you've drawn
the corpse of diamonds
for the third time.

PRIMOGENITURE

My dad beat me with his belt
for my edification and further

improvement and later that other
stranger took over

somewhat more expertly
which both learned from their fathers

some heavily armed
monkeys, from Plato's cave

to Darwin's— . . .
So that's how it is done

here,
I thought

and may my hand wither

may it forget how to write
if I ever strike a child.

MOVING

You were gone love
voice invisible
presence

for lack of which
welling up
          how would I live

No lightbulbs
And how would I write
without
light

corner of Nowhere and Everywhere, I swear

on my own grave
I'll never move again

PLANTING

The table set
the endless
table
set inside
the seed

It's not
what goes into
your mouth that defiles you but
what comes out of it

On second thought
the definitely finite
places set

There will only have been
so many of us

PC LULLABY

Martian polar storm as seen

in blue light with sound of the wind there

Recording of a Chinese bird bone flute 9,000 years ago

This is better than looking at pictures of gorging
nineteen-year-old vaginas

Your human blood under my fingernail soul-

black dawn of these streets gorgeously empty yes

It is still

dark out still snowing

You are still here still asleep

DYING THOUGHT NEAR THE SUMMIT

Apples have wings, true or false.

And this is just one place, one
time

EMPTY STAGE

My name is Franz, and I'm a recovering asshole.
I'm a ghost
that everyone can see;
one of the rats
who act
like they own the place.

CLARIFICATION

Someone once told me about a Buddhist
monk who on awakening

each morning said, "Master!"
Then he would answer

"Yes, master?" And then
in a loud voice demand

"Become sober!"
Listen to what I am saying,

but listen especially
to what I'm not saying—

Of all the powers of love,
this: it is possible

to die; which means
it's possible to live.

Now it is possible to die
without being mad or afraid.

NOTHINGSVILLE, MN

The sole tavern there, empty
and filled
with cigarette smoke;
the smell
of beer, urine, and the infinite
sadness you dread
and need so much of
for some reason

Franz Wright, the son of the poet James Wright, was born in Vienna in 1953. He grew up in the Northwest, the Midwest, and northern California. He is the recipient of two National Endowment for the Arts grants, a Whiting Fellowship, a Guggenheim Fellowship, and the PEN/Voelcker Award for Poetry, among other honors. He lives in Waltham, Massachusetts, with his wife, Elizabeth.

A NOTE ON THE TYPE

This book was set in Monotype Dante, a typeface designed by Giovanni Mardersteig (1892–1977). Conceived as a private type for the Officina Bodoni in Verona, Italy, Dante was originally cut only for hand composition by Charles Malin, the famous Parisian punch cutter, between 1946 and 1952. Its first use was in an edition of Boccaccio's *Trattatello in Laude di Dante* that appeared in 1954. The Monotype Corporation's version of Dante followed in 1957. Although modeled on the Aldine type used for Pietro Cardinal Bembo's treatise *De Aetna* in 1495, Dante is a thoroughly modern interpretation of the venerable face.

Composed by NK Graphics,
Keene, New Hampshire
Printed and bound by Edwards Brothers,
Ann Arbor, Michigan
Designed by Virginia Tan